Near Eastern and Classical Antiquities

J. Rossiter

D. Dillenbeck

The University of Alberta Press

Near Eastern and Classical Antiquities

*A Guide to the Antiquities Collection of the
Department of Classics at the University of Alberta*

compiled by
J. J. Rossiter and
D. E. Dillenbeck
*with an appendix on
Greek and Roman coinage
by* T. N. Ballin

University of Alberta Press

First published by
The University of Alberta Press
Edmonton, Alberta, Canada

1976

The funding for research, design, and publication of this book
was largely provided by the University Collections Committee
with assistance from the Faculty of Arts.

The book design, cover
design, illustrations, and
photography were executed
by Chi Lee, Susan Nash,
Michael Popowicz, and Bob
Robertson.

Printed in Canada by
Printing Services of The University of Alberta

Contents

Introduction

The collection of antiquities to which this catalogue serves as a guide is on display in the Department of Classics at the University of Alberta. As the title indicates, the material is drawn in part from the early cultures of the Near East, and in part from the civilisations of Greece and Rome. Thus the items represent a time span of some four thousand years, and provide us with an understanding of man's creative ability and technical skills at different periods in the long evolution of Western civilisation. The earliest objects are from southern Iraq, the products of a preliterate community of the fourth millennium BC. Following this is a collection of artifacts from Palestine, acquired from the excavation of an Iron-Age hill town near Jerusalem. The remaining objects are from the Greek and Roman periods.

The collection has been acquired gradually from a variety of sources. Some of the objects, including much of the Greek painted pottery, have been purchased; but many have been donated. For the Near Eastern material, a particular debt of gratitude is owed to Mrs. Margaret Judge, who in 1964 presented the University with a collection of antiquities which had belonged to her brother, the Rev. Dr. J.M. Menzies (1885-1957). Menzies worked for many years overseas as a missionary, and in 1929 was in the Near East. While he was in Palestine he served for a short period on the staff of the American excavation of Tell en-Nasbeh, and as a result of this and his visits to other Near Eastern countries, he acquired a sizeable collection of archaeological material. A selection of this material forms part of this exhibition. Most of the glass objects were obtained in 1954 by Dr. G.W. Hardy, from the trustees of the Norton collection of antiquities in Boston. The department is grateful to Dr. G. Hermansen through whose kindness many of the Roman bronze coins were acquired.

The authors would like to express their thanks to those who have helped in the preparation of this catalogue; Dr. D. Lubell, Dr. J.G. Schovanek, and especially Dr. A.M. Small, for his advice on many aspects of the work, in particular in connection with the

Greek pottery. The section on the Greek pottery was compiled jointly by the authors, that on the coins by Diane Dillenbeck; the rest was written by Jeremy Rossiter. Thanks also are due to the Palestine Institute of the Pacific School of Religion at Berkeley, California, for permission to reproduce the section drawing from the Tell en-Nasbeh excavation report; also to the University Collections Committee, and to the University Press, without whose co-operation this catalogue would not have been possible.

Part One
Near Eastern Antiquities

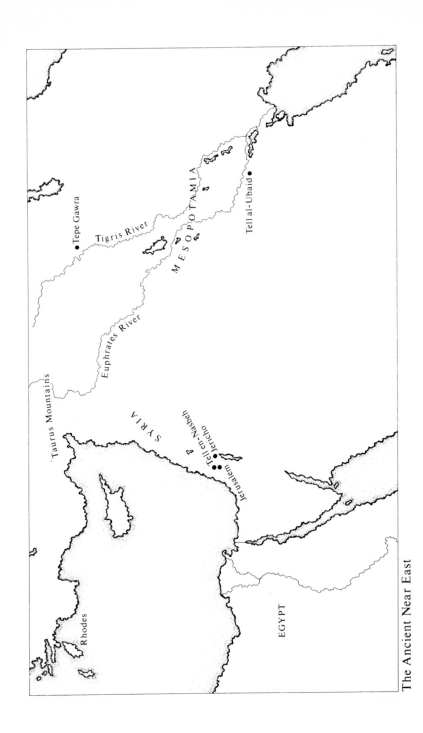

The Ancient Near East

Tell al-Ubaid
Iraq

In an archaeological context the word 'tell' denotes a hill or mound composed of the ruins of an ancient settlement. Tell al-Ubaid is the name of a small mound about four miles northwest of Ur, near the Euphrates river in south Iraq. Excavation of the site between 1919 and 1924 by H.R. Hall and Sir Leonard Woolley brought to light the remains of a distinctive culture which flourished there during the last part of the fifth and much of the fourth millennium BC.[1] Subsequent excavation at numerous sites elsewhere in Iraq has produced artifacts of a type similar to those found at Tell al-Ubaid, and shown that this culture, known after its original findspot as the Ubaid culture, at one time extended over a wide area of ancient Mesopotamia.

The Ubaid culture is one of the so-called 'protohistoric' cultures of ancient Iraq, which flourished during the period before the birth of literate civilisation at the end of the fourth millenium BC. These cultures represent a stage in the evolution of human society, before the invention of writing, when man, having acquired basic manufacturing skills, was beginning to give his artifacts a characteristic, often decorative quality, which enables us to differentiate between the products of a number of different cultural groups. The origin of the Ubaid culture is still obscure; it seems to have evolved to a certain extent from its predecessor in southern Iraq, the Hajji Muhammed culture, but was also probably carried by invasion or migration from south-west Iran.[2] Having taken root in the south of Iraq, its influence gradually spread northwards up the river valleys of the Tigris and Euphrates, ultimately extending as far as the Taurus Mountains in eastern Turkey.

The apparent prosperity of the Ubaid people probably stems from their effective systems of agriculture and irrigation. Excavation has brought to light many artifacts which illustrate their primitive agricultural technology. Their farm implements were made generally either of stone or clay. The numerous flint and obsidian blades of this period indicate the use of composite blade tools, such as knives and sickles, made by attaching a number of stone blades to a wooden handle, using bitumen as an adhesive. Particularly characteristic of the Ubaid culture are certain clay implements like the crescent-shaped sickles and cylindrical grinders. The rounded nail-shaped clay objects, which at one time were thought to be clay nails or decorative 'wall-cones', are more probably 'mullers' or pestles used for pounding.[3]

In the field of architecture important advances were made by the Ubaid people, especially in construction with mud-brick. The Ubaid temples at Tepe Gawra in north-east Iraq represent an impressive style of mud-brick architecture, which illustrates one of the finest achievements of the Ubaid people.[4] Such buildings were doubtless the focal points of the settlements and suggest that organised religion played a significant role in Ubaid society. Another characteristic feature of the culture is the decorative pottery which was produced during this period. This is of a distinctive if not highly imaginative appearance. The clay is usually buff, sometimes overfired to a greenish colour, and the decoration generally consists of simple geometric patterns in a dark brown or black.

□ *Indicates plate*

1 *Flint scraper*
(probably Palaeolithic)
shows signs of having been
reworked at a later date
L 10.0 cm
al-Ubaid

2 *Part of a backed chert blade*
L 3.2 cm
al-Ubaid
4th millennium BC

3 *Flint core*
from which flakes have been
removed
L 3.0 cm
al-Ubaid
4th millennium BC

4 *Part of a chalcedony blade*
cutting edge shows a
considerable 'sickle gloss',
acquired by prolonged use
to cut grasses
L 2.5 cm
al-Ubaid
4th millennium BC

5 *Flint blade*
retouched along edge by
use
L 4.5 cm
al-Ubaid
4th millennium BC

6 *Geometric microlith*
part of a flint blade, broken
deliberately to form a
rectangular tool, retouched
on all four sides, long sides
serrated, slight traces of
sickle gloss

2.1 x 1.2 cm
provenance unknown

7 *Obsidian blades*
pressure-flaked with ground
platforms
L 3.5 and 2.6 cm
provenance unknown

8 *Decorated pottery sherds*
□ al-Ubaid
4th millennium BC

9 *Terracotta spindle whorls*
conoid, vertically perforated
al-Ubaid
4th millennium BC

10 *Terracotta pendant, flat
circular*
bored suspension hole
crudely impressed pattern
of circles is visible on front
face
D 6.5 cm
al-Ubaid
4th millenium BC[5]

11 *Part of a clay implement*
(nail-shaped)

probably a 'muller' or
pestle
al-Ubaid
4th millennium BC

12 *Parts of two clay sickles*
al-Ubaid
4th millennium BC

13 *Clay handles*
(probably sickles)
al-Ubaid
4th millennium BC

14 *Cylindrical clay object*
tapering towards each end
and bored longitudinally.
This probably rotated
around a wooden rod and
was used for grinding or
rolling
L 7.3 cm
al-Ubaid
4th millennium BC[6]

15 *Stone quern used for
milling*
al-Ubaid
4th millennium BC

References

[1] H.R. Hall and C.L. Woolley. *Al-Ubaid. Ur Excavations Vol. I*
London, 1927.
C.L. Woolley 'Excavations at Tell el-Ubaid' *Antiquities
Journal IV* (1924) pp. 329-346.
The Museum Journal, University of Pennsylvania XV (1924),
pp. 237-251.
[2] For general accounts of the history of this period, see:
J. Mellaart. *Earliest civilisations of the Near East*. London, 1965.

G. Roux. *Ancient Iraq.* London, 1964, pp. 67-71.

[3] Their function is debated. For interpretations, see D. Stronach. 'Excavations at Ras al-Amiya' *Iraq XXIII* (1961) p. 107.

[4] A.J. Tobler. *Excavations at Tepe Gawra II.* Philadelphia, 1950.

[5] cf. Tobler. *op. cit.* p. 196 Plate CLXXIII. fig. 46.

[6] cf. Stronach, *op. cit.* p. 136. Plate XLIX. 1. bottom.

Tell en-Nasbeh
Palestine

The excavation

Tell en-Nasbeh is situated on high ground about six miles north of Jerusalem. It lies just west of the main road which runs northwards from Jerusalem along the watershed between the coastal plains of the Mediterranean and the Jordan valley. The site has long been recognised as that of an ancient settlement. In 1856 Edward Robinson described the meagre visible remains: *'merely the foundations of a tower with heaps of unwrought stones and fragments of pottery strowed about'*. The site was systematically excavated between 1926 and 1935 by F.W. Badè under the auspices of the Palestine Institute of the Pacific School of Religion and the American School of Oriental Research.[1] The excavation was carried out with commendable technical ability and in its day set exemplary standards. However, by modern standards the archaeological techniques used at Tell en-Nasbeh appear understandably antiquated.[2] The theory of stratigraphic excavation, that is excavation which observes and distinguishes the differences in soil strata and records all finds in the context of their soil levels, was not unknown to the excavators, but the technique by which this theory could be applied was still in its infancy. However, the systematic treatment of the finds once they had been extracted from the earth deserves much credit. The organised approach to every aspect of recording and the careful classification of the finds, give the Tell en-Nasbeh excavation a deserved place in the evolution of scientific archaeological technique.

The history of the site

The site of Tell en-Nasbeh was first occupied towards the end of the fourth millennium BC, between c 3250 and 3000 BC. At this time it seems that waves of migrant tribesmen entered Palestine from the north and east, coming especially along the route that leads from the east by way of Jericho.[3] They began to lead a sedentary existence in small communities, and from this the period of their occupation has been labelled the 'Proto-urban' period in Palestine. The name implies a stage in the emergence of settled civilised life before the development of urban communities in any real sense. So far three distinct groups of peoples from this period have been identified and it seems that these groups, although probably they entered the area at different times, came eventually to live side by side and to mingle their cultures. They lived in primitive, loosely organized village settlements, which were unwalled and have left virtually no trace of their architecture. One of the few things that we know about these peoples is the method by which they buried their dead, for the excavated material of this period comes largely from their tombs. At Tell en-Nasbeh two adjoining hillside caves (Cave-tombs 5 and 6) were used as large communal tombs for a number of successive multiple burials. Each was found to contain the skeletal remains of a number of bodies accompanied by pottery vessels, which originally would have contained such things as food and drink and perfume to provide for the departed on their final journey. The contents of the vessels have long since perished, but many of the vessels have survived, often intact, and serve as a valuable source of information for the archaeologist. By examining such vessels, their shape, fabric, and decoration, the archaeologist can begin to draw up a classification of pottery types which form a group representative of a particular culture or period. The pottery from the Proto-urban period at Tell en-Nasbeh is handmade and of a relatively crude appearance due largely to poor washing and firing of the clay.

At the end of the fourth millennium BC this first period of occupation came to an end, and the site was abandoned. It was not until the eleventh century BC that Tell en-Nasbeh again became a place of settled occupation. At this time the hill country of Palestine was occupied by Israelite and Canaanite tribes, while the coastal plains to the west were being settled by new invaders, the Philistines. The initial reoccupation of Tell en-Nasbeh was slight, probably no more than a village settlement. The following century, however (c 1030-930 BC), saw the consolidation and virtual unification of the Palestinian hill country under David and Solomon, and the rebuilding and refortification of many of the hill towns. It is probable that an early fortification wall at Tell en-Nasbeh belongs to this century. The division of Solomon's kingdom after c 930 BC led ultimately to the creation of two adjoining states in central Palestine, Israel to the north and Judah to the south. The new frontier between these two kingdoms lay just north of Jerusalem, passing near the site of Tell en-Nasbeh. The town naturally became one of renewed importance, a frontier post for Judah. It may perhaps be identified with the Biblical town of Mizpah. It is to the ninth and following centuries BC that the most formidable remains at Tell en-Nasbeh belong. The town walls were rebuilt and the town prospered, as the archaeological evidence clearly shows, for the excavations produced an abundance of material from these centuries, indicating a continuous and relatively prosperous occupation of the site. The political history of Palestine in this period (c 900-600 BC) is complex, a story of the gradual erosion of independence at the hands of the warring kings of Assyria and Babylonia as they sent their imperial armies westwards towards the Mediterranean. For Palestine this often meant the destruction of its towns and the enslavement of its people. Yet despite depredation elsewhere, urban life at Tell en-Nasbeh seems to have continued uninterrupted. Perhaps the townspeople were willing to submit their independence to Assyrian and Babylonian overlords without opposition in return for peace. By 587 BC the kingdom of Judah had become a province of the Babylonian empire. From that time until the time of Alexander the Great (died 323 BC), Palestine remained a subject state, first to the Babylonians and then to the Persians. The population of Tell en-Nasbeh began to decline in the fifth century BC, partly no doubt because the city had lost the strategic importance that it had attained as a frontier city of Judah. Although some late tombs indicate scattered settlement at the site during the Roman and Byzantine periods, the bulk of the archaeological material belongs to the period 900-500 BC.

The origin of the finds

The material extracted from an archaeological site normally derives from one of four sources: an occupation level, a destruction level, a burial deposit, or a rubbish pit. Finds from an occupation level are often of a fragmentary nature, the kind of waste that is trodden into the ground, such as animal bones, a pottery sherd, or a broken tool. Material from destruction levels is often the product of violent collapse, caused perhaps by an earthquake, or by fire, and therefore is often charred and broken. Burial deposits and rubbish pits, on the other hand, usually provide the archaeologist with more complete materials. In the case of the former, ancient burial custom often demanded the placing of vessels containing various provisions with the body in the tomb. Rubbish pits may contain vessels which are only partially broken, a jug without a handle, or perhaps a lamp with a broken spout.

Accordingly, at Tell en-Nasbeh the best preserved finds come from burial deposits and rubbish pits.[4] During the major phase of occupation from the ninth to the sixth century BC, a great many burials at Tell en-Nasbeh were made in cave-tombs or rock-cut tombs. Some of these, although plundered for metal objects at some period in history, were found to contain a large amount of pottery, much of it still intact. Other accumulations of pottery were discovered in disused cisterns and grain storage pits which had been filled with discarded objects.

The serial numbers cited below refer to items listed in Volume II of the Tell en-Nasbeh excavation report.

□ *Indicates plate*

16 *Handmade ampulla*
small ear-shaped juglet in
light yellow-brown clay, the
neck is made from a
separate piece of clay
wet-smoothed
H 7.5 cm
Tell en-Nasbeh
c 3250-3000 BC,
cf. TN/S.207

17 *Handmade vessel*
single handle, possibly a cup
light orange-brown clay with
scattered grey and white
grits
H 8.5 cm

Tell en-Nasbeh
c 3250-3000 BC

18 *Three handles from
handmade jars*
('pinch-lapped' type)
clay is pinched out and then
turned upwards and pressed
down on itself again
Tell en-Nasbeh
c 3250-3000 BC
cf. TN/S.123-4

Section from Tell en-Nasbeh

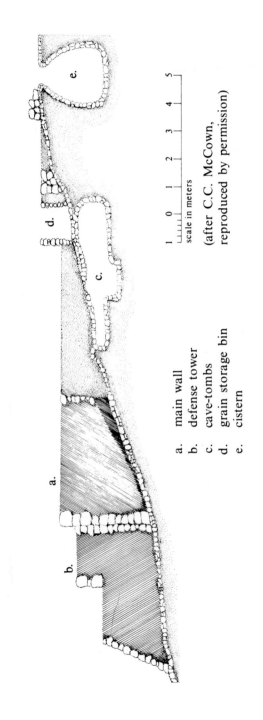

scale in meters

(after C.C. McCown,
reproduced by permission)

a. main wall
b. defense tower
c. cave-tombs
d. grain storage bin
e. cistern

Terracotta figurines

These figurines are of two types, either the image of a fertility goddess (Astarte), or of an animal. They seem to have been used as household icons and were kept in the home. Many were found broken at the neck and doubtless played a part in religious ritual, perhaps in rites of fertility magic.[5]

19 □ *Head of an Astarte figurine*
orange-brown clay, head has been pinched by hand and a superimposed band of clay indicates some sort of head-dress
H 3.7 cm
Tell en-Nasbeh
c 700-500 BC

20 □ *Torso of an Astarte figurine*
light orange-brown clay, one breast has been smashed, perhaps ritually, left arm is missing
H 5.8 cm
Tell en-Nasbeh
c 700-500 BC

21 *Head of an animal figurine*
(perhaps of a dog or a bull)
pinkish-brown clay coated with a white slip
H 6.2 cm
Cistern 173, Tell en-Nasbeh
c 700-500 BC

22 *Head of an animal figurine*
orange-red clay, eyes are applied in relief
H 4.2 cm
Tell en-Nasbeh
c 700-500 BC

23 *Body of an animal figurine*
pinkish-buff clay with grey core
broken at the neck and missing two legs
L 6.8, W 4.0, H 3.3 cm
Cistern 173, Tell en-Nasbeh
c 700-500 BC

---

24 □ *Part of a single-handled jug*
trefoil spout, yellowish brown clay, contains many tiny white grits
Tomb 5, Tell en-Nasbeh
c 900-600 BC

25 *Spout of a strainer jug*
yellow-brown clay
Tell en-Nasbeh
c 900-600 BC
cf TN/S.620-2

26 *Part of a two-handled pot*
light brown clay, grey core, greenish weathering on outside surface, neck is narrow, two pierced vertical

lug handles on the shoulder
D approx. 10.0 cm
Tell en-Nasbeh
c 900-600 BC
cf TN/S.1689

27 *Single-handled juglet*
grey-black clay, outside
surface is vertically
burnished, handle is missing
H 7.5+ cm
Tomb 5, Tell en-Nasbeh
c 900-600 BC
cf TN/S.858

28 *Ovoid single-handled juglet*
reddish-brown and buff clay,
contains some white grits,
broken handle and neck
H 8.2 cm
Tell en-Nasbeh
c 530-330 BC

29 *Single-handled juglet*
Reddish-brown clay, heavily
weathered, traces of a red
slip, broken handle and neck
H 9.0 cm
Tell en-Nasbeh
c 530-330 BC
cf TN/S.771

30 *Part of a single-handled
juglet*
grey-brown clay, numerous

tiny white grits
H 12.7+ cm
Palestine
c 600-400 BC

31 *Single-handled jug*
□ orange-brown clay, outside
surface and inside of the
neck are covered with a red
slip
H 11.5+ cm
Cistern 276, Tell en-Nasbeh
c 700-500 BC
cf TN/S.608

32 *Single-handled jug*
light orange-brown clay,
some small white grits, no
pouring lip, bottom of the
vessel is broken
H 21.0+ cm
Cistern 176, Tell en-Nasbeh
c 750-650 BC
cf TN/S.564

33 *Single-handled jug*
light brown clay, outside
surface light pinkish-brown
and wet-smoothed
H 22.0+ cm
Cistern 176, Tell en-Nasbeh
c 750-650 BC
cf TN/S.548

Pottery lamps

This series of pottery lamps from Palestine dates between c 900
and 500 BC. During this period the design of the lamp, essentially
a container for oil into which a wick could be placed, shows a

development from the earlier saucer lamp to the high-footed type. The earliest lamps consisted of no more than a shallow bowl with part of the rim pinched to form a spout. This left much of the wick exposed, and tended to produce a smoky flame. A cleaner flame was produced by the later lamps, on which the spout was pinched closely, almost forming a bridge, thus limiting the part of the wick which could burn.

34 *Saucer lamp*
☐ light yellow-brown clay, contains numerous tiny white grits, flat turned-back rim, rounded bottom
L 13.4 cm
Tomb 5, Tell en-Nasbeh
c 900-600 BC
cf TN/S.1618

35 *Part of a saucer lamp*
light yellow-brown clay, contains scattered white grits, flat turned-back rim, rounded bottom
L 12.5 cm
Tomb 5, Tell en-Nasbeh
c 900-600 BC
cf TN/S.1616

36 *High-footed lamp*
reddish-brown clay, smoked

spout
L 11.6 cm, H 5.5 cm
Cistern 176, Tell en-Nasbeh
c 700-500 BC
cf TN/S.1640

37 *High-footed lamp*
reddish-brown clay, contains scattered white grits
L 11.5 cm, H 6.0 cm
Tell en-Nasbeh
c 700-500 BC
cf TN/S.1637

38 *High-footed lamp*
☐ dark reddish-brown clay, closely pinched spout
L 8.9 cm, H 4.6 cm
Nazareth, Palestine
c 700-500 BC

---

39 *A group of stone sling-bolts*
Tell en-Nasbeh
late Iron Age

40 *Part of a bowl*
dark grey clay, scattered white grits, pinkish-brown surface, changing to yellow-brown at the top of the

outside face, disc base
D of rim 12.0 cm, H 5.0 cm
Cistern 176, Tell en-Nasbeh
c 700-500 BC
cf TN/S.1214

41 *Part of a shallow bowl*
yellow-buff clay
D 18.3 cm

Tomb 4, Tell en-Nasbeh
c 1st century BC

References

[1] For the excavation reports, see: C.C. McCown *Tell en-Nasbeh. Vol. I (Archaeological and Historical Results).* Berkeley, 1947. For the pottery, see: J.C. Wampler *Tell en-Nasbeh. Vol. II.* Berkeley, 1947.
W.F. Badè *Palestine Institute Publications, No. 1: Excavations at Tell en-Nasbeh 1926-27.* Berkeley, 1928.

[2] For excavation techniques, see: W.F. Badè *A manual of excavation in the Near East.* Berkeley, 1934.

[3] A general history of Palestine at this period is contained in Kathleen M. Kenyon *Archaeology in the Holy Land* (3rd edition) London, 1970.

[4] For an early report on the material from the tombs, see: W.F. Badè *Palestine Institute Publications, No. 2: Some tombs of Tell en-Nasbeh, discovered in 1929.* Berkeley, 1931.

[5] McCown *op. cit.* pp. 245-248.

Part Two
Classical Antiquities

Pottery

The history of Greek painted pottery is a long and complex one, spanning many centuries and involving many changes of style. The pottery vessels in this collection represent only a few of the many different styles of form and decoration which were produced at different periods in the various parts of the Greek world.

The earliest piece is a small Mycenaean feeding bottle [No. 43], which dates from between 1400 and 1200 BC. At this time mainland Greece was dominated by a number of independent warrior states, of which Mycenae, the fabled home of the king Agamemnon, was apparently one of the strongest and wealthiest.

From a much later period of Greek civilisation come the group of objects numbers 45 to 48. During the period of Greek colonial expansion (roughly 750-550 BC) the city of Corinth became one of the leading commercial cities of Greece, extending her trade and colonial ambitions to many parts of the Mediterranean. During these centuries Corinth was the major producer of exported pottery in Greece. She developed a distinctive style of pottery which reached its fullest form between c 625 and 550 BC. This so-called 'Ripe Corinthian' style is characterised by its pale yellowish clay and black-figure decoration (see appendix i), commonly in the form of animal designs, with additional filling ornament such as palmette and rosette motifs. The painted additions in white and shades of red and purple are another feature of this style of ornament.

During the first part of the sixth century BC, the commercial supremacy of Corinth was gradually eroded by the growth of Athens as an important trading power. By c 575 BC Athens had overtaken Corinth as the major producer of painted pottery. At this time the Athenian potters were working in their own style of black-figure design, in which they achieved a high degree of artistic skill. However, by c 530 BC a new style of decoration was introduced at Athens, which was essentially a reversal of the black-figure technique. This was the Attic red-figure style, in which the background was painted black while the figures were left in the colour of the clay. The details were applied to the figures with a fine brush, a technique which allowed for greater artistic delicacy than had the black-figure technique of incision. This style of decoration was popular in Athens for nearly two hundred years, though the quality of the painting began to decline towards the middle of the fifth century BC. The examples included here [Nos. 50 and 53], date from a relatively late phase of this style. The Athenian potteries by no means restricted themselves to the production of red-figure wares. Other styles of decoration were used, one of which was the so-called 'white-ground' style, in which figures were painted in outline on a white or cream background and enhanced with additional coloured washes. This type of decoration is represented here by the Attic white-ground lekythos [No. 54]. Plain black-glazed pottery [Nos. 51 and 52] was also produced, and formed an inexpensive table ware.

The production of red-figure pottery in south Italy, an area heavily colonised by the Greeks, began around the middle of the fifth century BC. Local styles, which were initially imitative of Attic red-figure, gradually developed their own characteristics. The application of subsidiary decoration became less restrained, and the use of additional colours increased. During the fourth and early third centuries a type of pottery was produced in south Italy which abandoned the red-figure technique altogether; this 'Gnathian' ware, in which the decoration is simply painted in colours onto a black ground, is illustrated by the squat lekythos [No. 56].

The group of stamped handles [Nos. 57-59] are from large wine-jars (*amphorae*) produced in Rhodes during the Hellenistic period. At this time the island of Rhodes was a major commercial centre, the extent of whose trade can be appreciated from the many locations in the Mediterranean where jars with stamps similar to these have been found.

☐ *Indicates plate*

42 *Mycenaean feeding bottle*　　　　H 11.8 cm
☐ decoration in umber on　　　　　1400-1200 BC
cream, angled spout, handle
arching over the filler hole,　　43 *Terracotta figurine*
chipped on one side　　　　　☐ mould-pressed, this figurine

is of the type known as
'Dedalic plaque' figurines,
style shows oriental
influence, probably derived
from Phoenician 'Astarte'
figurines
H 15.0 cm
Cretan
mid-7th century BC

44   *Squat amphora*
☐   Etruscan Bucchero
decoration consists of groups
of incised lines with a bird
above a double spiral at
each side
H 13.4 cm
c 670-650 BC[1]

45   *Alabastron*
☐   (small perfume bottle)
black-figure technique with
painted additions in red,
central design is of two cocks
facing each other, separated
by a lotus and palmette
motif, decoration is worn in
places
H 10.0 cm
Early Corinthian
c 625-600 BC[2]

46   *Pyxis*
☐   (small container with a lid

for cosmetics or trinkets)
buff with painted decoration
in dulled brown and red, lid
is chipped
H 5.0 cm
Early Corinthian
c 625-600 BC[3]

47   *Aryballos*
☐   used for oil or scent, neck is
narrow to reduce
evaporation
black-figure technique,
painted additions in purple,
on one side a swan, on the
other, a quadruple lotus
complex, chip from the
breast of the swan
H 11.6 cm
Middle Corinthian
c 600-575 BC[4]

48   *Aryballos*
black-figure technique
reddish-brown on cream,
design is of a siren with
spread wings, blotch at the
end of the nose is
presumably erroneous,
multiple horizontal lines at
neck and base
H 6.4 cm
Late Corinthian
c 575-550 BC[5]

49   *Lekane*
☐   Name given to this type of footed dish, with two recurving
handles and a flattened lip. Black figures on dull brown ground,
painted additions in red. Handle zone: series of water fowl.
Central zone: pairs of lions separated by siren. Stripes around
base, filling ornament including dot rosettes, swastikas with dots
in angles, and a cross with segments in angles. Interior black,

undecorated. Partially restored
H 6.8 cm, D 25.6 cm, Corinthianising, of uncertain origin
c 575-550 BC[6]

50 *Skyphos*
☐ (type of cup)
red-figure technique
on one side a running goat,
on the other, a running
satyr, one handle set
vertically, the other
horizontally,
colour differential of the
vessel is due to poor firing
H 7.9 cm
Attic
c 450-425 BC

51 *Ribbed one-handled mug*
☐ (Pheidias shape)
black glaze, underside
reserved, flat bottom,
decorated with two painted
black rings and a dot, thin
line of notching at the
junction of wall and neck
H 9.0 cm
Attic
450-425 BC[7]

52 *Bolsal*
☐ Name given to this type of
cup, with a wall which rises
vertically to a plain rim, a
ring base and two
horizontal handles.
Stamped design at the
centre of the inside surface,
consisting of a simple
palmette cross, black glaze,
underside reserved,
decorated with painted
black bands and circles
H 4.6 cm, D 9.7 cm
Attic
425-400 BC[8]

53 *Squat lekythos*
small pot used for perfume
or oil
red-figure technique,
decoration is sphynx with
raised wings (see cover
design)
H 7.9 cm
Attic
c 425-400 BC

54 *Lekythos*
☐ Flask for oil, made specially for use in funerary ritual. This is
an example of the class of 'white-ground' lekythoi produced in
Athens during the fifth century BC, for which a decoration in
outline, commonly with painted additions in different colours,
was applied over a background of a white or cream slip. Traces
of the design survive on this lekythos, and show a male figure
seated by a tomb
H 22.3 cm
Attic
450-425 BC

55 Cup
orange-buff with painted
decoration in black,
this type of cup is derived
from a series of Ionian cups
of the 6th century BC,
found in excavations at
Centuripe in Sicily in 1969
H 4.6 cm
probably 5th century BC
Donated by Dr. W.H. Johns

56 Squat lekythos
□ toilet vessel in 'Gnathian'
technique
decoration of a winged
Victory (the goddess Nike)
and subsidiary florid
vegetation, is applied in
white, yellow, and purple
paint to a black ground
H 10.6 cm
south Italian
c 350-325 BC

The Rhodian Amphora handles

Rhodian amphorae normally bore two stamps, one on each
handle. One gave the name of the magistrate (eponym) in whose
term of office the jar was made, the other the name of the
manufacturer. The former probably served as a licence to the
manufacturer; its use to date the contents of the jar (e.g. to
indicate the year of a vintage wine) would only apply if the jar
were filled soon after it had been made. The licence, and the
manufacturer's endorsement, were probably intended as
guarantees of standard capacity and quality.

57 Stamped amphora handle
giving the name of the
eponym and the month of
office:
ΕΠΙΘΑΡΣΙΠΟΛΙ/ΠΑΝΑΜΟΥ
('In the term of Tharsipolis,
in the month of Panamos')
Rhodian
found at Beit Jabrin,
Palestine
c 280-220 BC[9]

58 Stamped amphora handle
giving the name of the
manufacturer:
ΔAM ..../TIMOΓEN
('Dam. . . ., son of
Timogenes'), Rhodian
found at Beit Jabrin,
Palestine

59 Stamped amphora handle
showing head of Helios (the
sun god) in circle
surrounded by the name of

the eponym and the month
of office:
EΠI ANΔPON[IKON]
[AΓP]IANOY
('In the term of
Andron[icos], in the month
of [Agr]ianos'), secondary

stamp on the side of the
handle in form of small
square containing the letter
A, Rhodian
found at Beit Jabrin,
Palestine
c 150-100 BC[10]

---

60 *Loom weight*
stone, bored horizontally
near the top
H 9.5 cm
south Italian, Hellenistic

References

1 cf. T. Dohrn 'Die Etruskische Bandhenkelamphora des 7. Jh. v. Chr.' in *Studi in Onore di Luisa Banti*. Rome, 1965. pp. 143-152.
2 For parallel types see H. Payne *Necrocorinthia*. Oxford, 1931. pp. 282 Nos. 273-276.
3 cf. *ibid.* p. 292. Fig. 129. No. 665.
4 cf. *ibid.* pp. 303-305. (Round aryballoi, Type IIIB.)
5 cf. *ibid.* p. 321. (Flat-bottomed aryballoi, Type A. Nos. 1264-72.)
6 The filling ornament and the dull brown ground suggest a Corinthian derivative style
cf. the curious example of a lekanis quoted by R.J. Hopper in 'Addenda to Necrocorinthia' in *Annual of the British School at Athens No. XLIV* (1949) pp. 229-230.
7 cf. B.A. Sparks and L. Talcott. *The Athenian Agora, Vol. XII, Black and Painted Pottery* pp. 72-74. Pl. 11. No. 201.
8 cf. *ibid.* pp. 107-108. Pls. 24 and 53. No. 556.
9 The name occurs on stamps from Délos and Samaria, and the identification in all three cases is possible, although the likelihood of the name recurring should not be ignored.
cf. V. Grace 'Timbres amphoriques trouvés à Délos', *Bulletin de Correspondance Hellénique Vol. 76* (1952) p. 529.
J.W. Crowfoot, G.M. Crowfoot, K.M. Kenyon *Samaria-Sebaste III: The Objects*. London, 1957. p. 381.
10 cf. Grace *op. cit.* p. 528. Crowfoot *op. cit.* p. 380.

Glass

The survival of glass objects from antiquity in an undamaged state is often due to the fact that glass vessels formed a part of the grave-goods which, according to Roman custom, were placed in the tombs of the dead.[1] The majority of the glass items in this collection derive from tomb groups of the Roman period and would have served to contain unguents and provisions for the dead. Although most of the objects postdate the invention of glass-blowing, one vessel [No. 61] illustrates the earlier technique of 'core-dipping' (see appendix ii). It is most probably of Syrian manufacture, for it was mainly here that these small decorated unguent vessels were being produced during the fifth and fourth centuries BC. It was most probably in Syria too, towards the end of the first century BC, that the technique of glass-blowing was first discovered. The new technique transformed the glass industry; it meant that vessels could be produced more quickly than by earlier methods, and in a far greater variety of shapes. The technique spread rapidly. From the eastern Mediterranean skilled glass-blowers travelled to Italy, where they established glass-houses to provide for the western markets of the Roman world. By the end of the first century AD, glass was being produced in many parts of the Roman Empire. In the east, Syria and Egypt were the main centres of production, while in the west the spread of the industry into Gaul and Germany, and in particular to the Rhineland, is well attested.

□ *Indicates plate*

61 *Core-dipped amphoriskos*
□ dark blue matrix inlaid with
threads of opaque yellow
and light blue
H 7.3 cm
Phoenician
5th/4th century BC[2]

62 *Unguent bottle*
□ blown, purple, originally a
two-handled vessel, one
handle is missing, slightly
concave base, rim pulled out
and rolled over inwards
H 7.8 cm

probably early 1st century
AD

63 *Unguent bottle*
blown, dark green, flared
rim, flat base
H 11.3 cm
1st century AD

64 *Unguent bottle*
blown, dark green, thick
bubbly glass, rim pulled out,
rolled over inwards, concave
base
Egyptian manufacture
H 7.0 cm
1st/2nd century AD[3]

65 *Unguent bottle*
☐ blown, pale green, bell-
shaped body, with concave
base, flared rim,
patches of flaking especially
on base, very bubbly glass
on one side
H 17.5 cm
3rd century AD[4]

66 *Jug*
☐ blown, crook-shaped handle
attached at rim and
shoulder, surface highly
eroded and iridescent
flaring rim, edge rolled over
inwards, spiralling thread
added to neck
H 14.0 cm
Syrian manufacture
3rd/4th century AD[5]

67 *Beaker*
blown, clear glass, slightly

green tinge
patches of milky weathering,
flared rim, sides carinated
towards base, flat base
H 9.2 cm
2nd/3rd century AD

68 *Bowl*
blown, light green, heavy
flaking on inside surface,
solid ring base
Syrian manufacture
H 5.3 cm, D 9.0 cm
3rd/4th century AD

69 *Beaker*
☐ blown, light green, flaked
patches and surface
iridescence,
cylindrical body, slightly
concave sides, single blue-
green thread applied to
upper part of body
Syrian manufacture
H 11.5 cm
4th century AD[6]

70 *Double unguent bottle*
☐ blown, pale green, heavy
weathering and flaking
leaving iridescent surface,
small section of a loop
handle survives on one side
Syrian manufacture
H 10.5 cm
4th/5th century AD

71 *Unguent bottle*
blown, pale green body,
dark green base ring,
concave showing pontil
mark

probably Syrian
manufacture
H 10.8 cm
Medieval

72　*Rim fragment from a glass
bowl*
manganese purple glass
with marvered white threads
Islamic
10th/12th century AD[7]

References

[1] For this practice see J.M.C. Toynbee, *Death and Burial in the Roman World.* London, 1971. pp. 52-53.

[2] cf. Poul Fossing, *Glass Vessels before Glass Blowing,* 1940, pp. 71-72.

[3] cf. D.B. Harden. *Roman Glass from Karanis. University of Michigan Studies. Humanistic Series. Vol. XLI* (1936) p. 274. Class XIII C.

[4] cf. J.W. Crowfoot, G.M. Crowfoot, K.M. Kenyon, *Samaria— Sebaste III: The Objects.* London, 1957. p. 408, Fig. 94.1.

[5] For this type of Syrian jug cf. Crowfoot *op. cit.* p. 414, Fig. 96.9.

[6] cf. D.B. Harden. 'Tomb-groups of glass of Roman date from Syria and Palestine' *Iraq XI* (1949) p. 151, Fig. 1.

[7] cf. *Journal of Glass Studies XIII* (1971) p. 140, Fig. 33.

Lamps

These lamps represent different types produced between the third century BC and the sixth century AD. The designs of the lamps vary considerably in detail, but their essential components are the same: a tank for the oil, a filling hole, and a wick aperture. The differences in shape, in the treatment of the nozzle, and in the style and degree of decoration, reflect changing fashion and local taste. The introduction of moulded lamps in the third century BC, in place of the earlier wheel-made lamps, led to an increased amount of relief decoration, applied mainly to the top and shoulders of the lamp. Many of the more common Roman lamp forms were first produced in quantity in Italy and were subsequently copied, usually with less refinement, in provincial workshops.

□ *Indicates plate*

73 *Wheel-made lamp*
□ suspension lug at side, buff clay, dark reddish-brown glaze, some surface encrustation
cf. Howland Type 34A. No. 448
L 9.0, W 6.2, H 3.6 cm
3rd/2nd century BC

74 *Moulded lamp*
□ on the discus is a rough moulding of a couple. Buff clay with reddish-brown glaze
L 8.8, W 7.5, H 2.7 cm
1st/2nd century AD

75 *Moulded lamp*
partly broken filling-hole, Menorah motif on rear shoulders and handle, light orange-brown clay
L 7.2, W 5.5, H 3.5 cm
Palestine
5th/6th century AD

76 *Legionary tile-stamp*
□ (LEGIO X FRETENSIS) This legion was among those used to suppress the Jewish uprising (66-70 AD) which led to the

Roman destruction of Jerusalem. From this time until the end of the third century AD the legion was stationed at Jerusalem.

Coins

The coins listed here are a representative selection from a larger collection. Two are from Asiatic kingdoms of the Hellenistic period [No. 77, 78], while the remainder are Roman coins from the Republic and the Empire.

The emblems on ancient coins might either indicate the authority responsible for the issue of the coin, or they might serve as visual propaganda for that authority. On Hellenistic coins the obverse had a portrait of the ruling king, while the reverse often showed some aspect of the state religion. Portraits of living individuals were not represented on the earliest coins of the Roman Republic on which the heads represented Rome, personified as a goddess, or other gods [No. 79, 80]. By the late third century BC, however, the moneyers gradually began putting their names on the coins, and the name of Rome quickly disappeared from the legends [No. 81, 82]. During the first century BC the portraits of living generals occasionally appeared on the obverse, while the reverse was often given to self-advertisement of that general. This trend was developed further in the Imperial coinage which glorified the Emperor and the state.

The coinage of the Roman Republic was issued mainly to pay state expenses and was minted by the authority of the Senate. A college of moneyers, three elected minor officials, controlled the mints. The name, or names, of the moneyer would appear on almost all later Republican coins; one of those listed below [No. 82] bears the names of all three. Magistrates other than moneyers could be given special authority to strike coins, as for instance the Curule Aedile, Crassipes [No. 83].

Generals in the field would mint coins at mobile mints in order to provide pay for the armies without the dangers of transporting large amounts from Italy [No. 87]. Most of these military issues were probably not sanctioned by the Senate.

Roman Imperial coinage was minted by the authority of the Emperor. The gold and silver coins stressed the Emperor's military powers, while the other coins emphasised the civil powers of the Emperor and the state honours paid to him. Although the

Senate no longer controlled coinage, the letters SC (*senatus consultum*—decree of the Senate) were retained on many of the lower denominations of coinage through tradition. The obverse generally bore the portrait of the Emperor, while the reverse was devoted to a deity, or to the personification of a virtue, or referred to some important event such as a conquest. The coins customarily depict abstract concepts, such as justice, in human form. As there was a wide circulation of Imperial coinage throughout the Empire, the coins served as a useful means of propaganda for the Emperor and Rome.

The title 'Augustus' designated the ruling Emperor. The name 'Caesar' was originally that of the dynasty of Augustus and was used by subsequent Emperors or, from the time of Hadrian, by their designated successors. The parentage of the ruling Emperor, in many cases by adoption, was indicated by the name of his predecessor. A coin dedicated to an Emperor who had received divine worship would bear the inscription DIVVS (deified) [No. 88].

Relative values of Imperial Roman coinage

	aureus	
=	2 quinarii aurei	} gold
=	25 denarii	
=	50 quinarii argentei	} silver
=	100 sestertii	
=	200 dupondii	} orichalcum (brass)
=	400 asses	} copper

□ *Indicates plate*

77 *Bronze two-chalkoi*
obverse
Head of Antiochus IV
King of Syria

reverse
ΒΑΣΙΛΕΩΣ. ΑΝΤΙΟΧΟΥ.
(of King Antiochus)
Zeus Nikephoros
(bearing victory) on throne

Hellenistic coin minted probably at Seleucia, c 175-164 BC, Ref. Head, p. 762

78 *Silver drachm*
☐ *obverse*
Head of Mithridates II
King of Parthia

reverse
ΒΑΣΙΛΕΩΣ. ΒΑΣΙΛΕΩΝ.
ΜΕΓΑΛΟΥ. ΑΡΣΑΚΟΥ.
ΕΠΙΦΑΝΟΥΣ.
Arsaces the founder seated and
holding a bow

Translation of reverse: of the King of Kings, of great Arsaces
Epiphanes. Hellenistic coin minted in Parthia, c 127-88 BC,
Ref: Head, p. 819

79 *Silver victoriatus*
☐ *obverse*
Head of Jupiter

reverse
ROMA
Victory placing wreath on
trophy

Refers to the Roman conquest of Illyricum and Corcyra in
229 BC. Minted at Rome, c 205-195 BC, Ref: Craw 53/1

80 *Silver quinarius*
obverse
Helmeted head of Roma

reverse
ROMA
the Roman gods, Castor and
Pollux on horseback

Minted at Rome, c 187-175 BC, Ref: Craw 44/6

81 *Silver denarius*
obverse
Helmeted head of Roma

reverse
P. SVLA.ROMA
Victory in the two-horse chariot

Moneyer: Publius Cornelius Sulla, minted at Rome, c 151 BC,
Ref: Craw 205/1

82 *Silver denarius*
☐ *obverse*
Helmeted head of Roma

reverse
AP.CL.T.ML.Q.VR
Victory in a three-horse
chariot

Moneyer: Appius Claudius, Titus Mallius, Quintus Urbinius,
minted at Rome, c 111-110 BC, Ref: Craw 299/1a

83   Silver denarius
☐   *obverse*   *reverse*
Turreted female head   P. FOVRIVS.CRASSIPES
AED.CVR (*Aedilis Curulis*)   Curule chair
deformed foot

Head is probably Cybele, the great mother. Moneyer: Publius
Fourius Crassipes, Curule Aedile of the city. The deformed foot
is a symbol for his name (*crassipes* = 'fat foot'). Minted at Rome,
c 84 BC, Ref: Craw 356/1a

84   Silver denarius
☐   *obverse*   *reverse*
SALVTIS (Safety)   M.ACILIVS.III.VIR.VALEV
Head of Salus   Valetudo (Health) holding
                          snake in right hand, leaning
                          on a column

Moneyer: Manlius Acilius. Salus and Valetudo are almost
synonymous divinities. The snake is normally associated with
divinities connected with healing (cf. no. 92). The first Greek
doctor was supposedly introduced to Rome by the Acilius
family. Minted at Rome, c 49 BC, Ref: Craw 442/16

85   Silver denarius
☐   *obverse*   *reverse*
CAESAR   *Culullus, aspergillum*, axe
Elephant trampling dragon,   and apex
symbolizes victory over evil   Emblems of the office of
                          Pontifex Maximus, the
                          chief priesthood, held by
                          Caesar

Private issue of Julius Caesar glorifying his recent conquests in
Gaul. Minted in Gaul, c 49-48 BC, Ref: Craw 443/1

86   Silver denarius
☐   *obverse*   *reverse*
Head of Apollo   P.CLODIVS.M.F.
lyre behind   Diana Lucifera (light-bearing)
                          lighted torch in each hand

One role of Apollo was as a god of music. Apollo and Diana
represent the contrast of the sun and the moon. Moneyer: Publius
Clodius. Minted at Rome, c 42 BC, Ref: Craw 494/23

87 *Silver denarius*
☐ *obverse*   *reverse*
ANT.AVG.III.VIR.R.P.C.   LEG. VIII
galley bearing standard above   *Aquila* between two *signa*
prow

Inscription of the obverse translates Antonius, *Augur* (religious
official who interprets omens). *Triumvir rei publicae constituendae*
(Triumvir for setting the state in order). *Aquila* (legionary
standard bearing the eagle and number of the legion). *Signa*
(military standards). Coin of the eighth legion issued by Marcus
Antonius (Mark Antony) prior to the battle of Actium in 31 BC.
Minted at mobile mint in the East, c 32-31 BC, Ref: Craw 544/21

88 *Copper as*
☐ *obverse*   *reverse*
DIVVS.AVGVSTVS.PATER.   S.C.
Head of Augustus   Eagle standing on globe

The eagle represents the soul of the deified Emperor, Augustus.
Commemorative coin struck by Tiberius. Minted at Rome,
c 16-22 AD, Ref: BMC 155

89 *Copper as*
☐ *obverse*   *reverse*
NERO.CAESAR.AVG.   S.C.
GERM.IMP.   Victory holding a shield
Head of Nero   inscribed S.P.Q.R.

Nero Caesar Augustus Germanicus (conqueror of Germany),
Emperor. The shield represents that originally conferred on
Augustus by the Senate and the Roman people (S.P.Q.R.) in
recognition of his great virtues, which Nero claims to possess.
Minted at Rome, c 64-66 AD, Ref: BMC 241

90 *Orichalcum dupondius*
obverse   *reverse*
IMP.CAES.NERVAE.   S.P.Q.R. OPTIMO.
TRAIANO.AVG.GER.DAC.P.   PRINCIPI (best of rulers)
M.TR.P.COS.V.P.P.   S.C. Legionary *aquila* between
Head of Trajan   two *signa*

(Imperatori Caesari Nervae Traiano Augusto Germanico Dacico,
Pontifici Maximo, Tribunicia Potestate, Consuli V, Patri Patriae.)
This coin is in honour of the Emperor Trajan, son of Nerva,

conqueror of Germany, conqueror of Dacia, Pontifex Maximus, with tribunician power, consul for the fifth time, Father of the country. The Emperor Nerva had adopted Trajan. Minted at Rome, c 104-111 AD, Ref: BMC 946A

91 *Copper as*
☐ *obverse*
HADRIANVS.AVG.COS.
III.P.P.
Head of Hadrian

reverse
ANNONA.AVG.S.C.
Annona holding ears of corn in right hand, rudder in left

Hadrianus Augustus, Consul for the third time, Father of the country. Personification of the corn supply provided by the Emperor. Minted at Rome, c 134-138 AD, Ref: BMC 1578

92 *Copper as*
obverse
IMP.CAES.M.AVREL.
ANTONINVS
AVG.P.M.
Head of Marcus Aurelius

reverse
SALVTI.AVGVSTOR.TR.P.
XVII.S.C.
COS.III
Salus feeding snake, holding sceptre in left hand

Minted at Rome c 163 AD, Ref: BMC 1046

93 *Bronze follis*
☐ *obverse*
CONSTANTINVS.P.F.AVG.
Head of Constantine the Great

reverse
SOLI.INVICTO.COMITI.
(to the unconquered Sun, the companion)
Sol (the Sun) with globe in left hand

(*Pius Felix*—pious and fortunate.) Minted at Lyons, c 313-314 AD, Ref: RIC 5

References

M.H. Crawford, *Roman Republican Coinage, Vols. I and II.* Cambridge, 1974.
B.V. Head, *Historia Numorum.* London, 1963.
H. Mattingly, *Coins of the Roman Empire in the British Museum, Vols. I-III.* London, 1968.

C. Sutherland and R. Carson, editors, *The Roman Imperial Coinage,* London, 1966.

Technical Appendices

Pottery Techniques

In studying ancient pottery we need to examine three things: the fabric, the decoration, and the shape. The first of these depends upon the type of clay being employed and the way in which this is prepared and fired. The clay is very often mixed with a filler, that is a strengthening agent such as quartz-grit or pulverised flint, which serves to prevent the pottery from cracking when in the kiln. The type of filler used can be an important factor in the identification of pottery clay. The colour of the pottery after firing will vary according to the chemical analysis of the clay and the conditions of the firing.

There are various techniques whereby the surface of a pottery vessel may be treated. Two of the simplest means of enhancing the appearance of a vessel are the processes known as burnishing and wet-smoothing. The former involves the rubbing down of the surface of a partially dried pot with a smooth object such as a bone or a water-worn pebble, in order to compact the surface clay. In the case of the latter, the surface is rubbed with a damp cloth or a wet finger. Another possible process is the application of what is termed a slip. This is a liquid suspension of clay and water into which the pot may be dipped before firing. This coats the surface with a thin ceramic film, often of a colour different to that of the body clay. A very thin slip is sometimes referred to as a wash.

Surface decoration may be either plastic or graphic. If the potter wishes to decorate his pot in the former manner, he may use such techniques as incision, or impression. Alternatively, the vessel may be cast in a mould to give a pattern in relief. This was the process adopted for Roman Sigillata ware; here a clay mould was made and the decorative motifs were applied to the inside of the mould by means of baked-clay stamps. In the case of graphic decoration, the design is painted onto the surface of the pot. The most celebrated painted pottery wares in antiquity were the Greek black- and red-figure wares.

The creation of these types of painted pottery involved special techniques. The clay used by most Greek potters had a high iron oxide content. This meant that a difference in firing atmosphere in the kiln would produce a difference in clay colour. In a clean, or oxidising atmosphere, the clay will fire to a reddish colour, whereas in a smoky, reducing atmosphere the same clay will turn black. Moreover, if refined in the form of a solution, this clay will change more slowly when fired. To create his design the painter applied a solution of the clay to those parts of the surface of the pot which he intended to be black—in the case of black-figure pottery, to the body of the projected figures, in the case of the red-figure, to the background. At this stage there was a variation in appearance, not in colour but in tone, between the clay of the body and the clay of the solution. The details of the figures were then applied, in the black-figure technique by incision with a sharp tool, in the red-figure by the additional painting of fine lines. Patches of colour could also be added if desired, the commonest being purple and white. These colours were formed by making up clay solutions with specific pigments. To achieve the correct colour contrast required careful firing.

There were three stages in the firing process. First the kiln was given a clean, oxidising atmosphere and the temperature gradually raised to about 800°C, until the whole surface of the pot was fired red. Secondly, the atmosphere was made smoky and the temperature raised to about 950°C, until the surface turned black. Thirdly, the temperature was lowered and an oxidising atmosphere was again created. The pottery began to turn red again, but where the paint had been applied the surface did not change colour so quickly. At the correct moment, when the body was again red and the applied paint still black, the kiln was allowed to cool and the pot removed.

Pottery vessels are also classified according to their shape. The names given to these shapes are for the most part conventional. Some have modern equivalents, and their names immediately convey a recognisable image such as a cup or a bowl. For others there are no modern equivalents and names extracted from ancient literature and lexicons have been applied to them. The more common of these shapes are illustrated below.

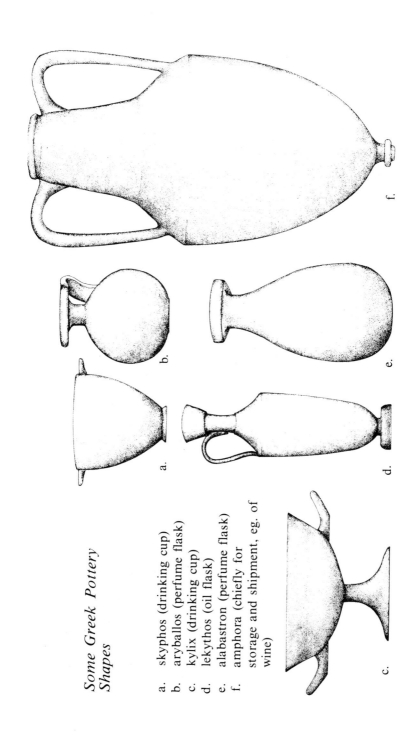

Some Greek Pottery Shapes

a. skyphos (drinking cup)
b. aryballos (perfume flask)
c. kylix (drinking cup)
d. lekythos (oil flask)
e. alabastron (perfume flask)
f. amphora (chiefly for storage and shipment, eg. of wine)

Glass Manufacturing

Before the invention of glass-blowing in the late first century BC, most glass vessels were made by a process known as *core-dipping*. A core, either of clay, or more commonly of sand contained within a cloth bag, was attached to the end of a rod and then dipped into a crucible of molten glass. Upon removal, the vessel which had been formed around the core was rolled on a flat surface (*marvered*) to help shape it; also coloured decoration could be added by applying trails of different coloured glass to the outside and marvering these into the surface to produce simple wave and zig-zag patterns. The main centre of production for these core-dipped vessels during the last few centuries BC was Phoenicia, and from here they were exported to many parts of the Mediterranean.

Other techniques in use at this time included *cold-cutting* and *mould-pressing*. In the case of the former an object was fashioned from a solid block of glass. This technique was used to produce cut-glass gems, and as such was similar to the cutting and grinding techniques applied to precious stones. The skills of the glass-cutter could also be used to fashion vessels, but such a process was slow and was used mainly to produce quality glass wares, such as were made at Alexandria in Egypt in the Hellenistic period. Glass cutting and grinding techniques were commonly used as a secondary process to decorate mould-pressed glass vessels, made simply by pressing viscous glass into a prepared mould.

The invention of glass-blowing quickly outdated all these earlier methods. The new process was quicker and could be used to create a far greater variety of shapes. The technique of glass-blowing can be summarised as follows: the blower takes a gob of molten glass on the end of a hollow blow-pipe, an iron tube about three to five feet long and between half-an-inch and one inch in diameter. This he inflates so that the glass forms a bulb, which can then be worked to the required shape by marvering on a flat surface, or tooling with pliers. A solid iron rod (the *pontil* or *punty*) is then attached to the bottom of the vessel with the aid

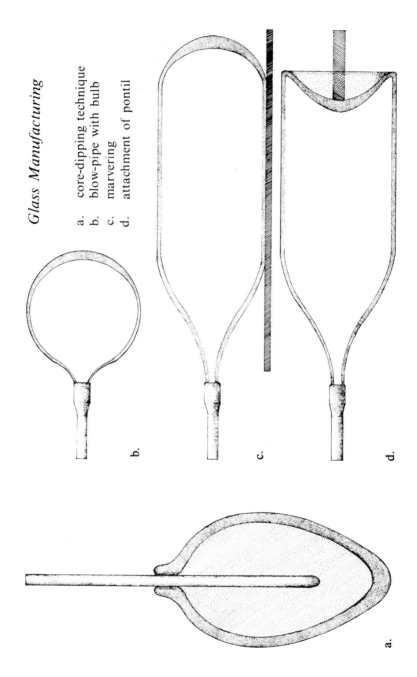

Glass Manufacturing

a.   core-dipping technique
b.   blow-pipe with bulb
c.   marvering
d.   attachment of pontil

of a glass seal so that the blow-pipe can be removed and the neck and rim fashioned. To make a bowl or beaker the bulb is cut with shears to form an open rim. The pontil is then detached and the vessel allowed to cool very gradually to reduce internal stress. Sometimes vessels were made by blowing the glass into a mould, usually designed to give the vessel a pattern in relief. The decoration for free-blown glasses could be produced in a variety of ways. Threads or blobs of viscous glass were sometimes fused to the outside of the vessel while it was held on the blow-pipe or pontil. Alternatively a thread, having been applied to the surface of the vessel, could be inlaid by reheating the glass and marvering it. Such applied and inlaid threads were often of a different colour to the glass of the main body.

The colour of glass depends on the chemical ingredients of the glass metal, in particular on the amount of metal oxides present. The greenish tint common to much ancient glass results from the presence of iron oxides in the sand or silicates from which it is made. This tint can be counteracted by the addition of manganese dioxide or antimony; in the Roman period the use of manganese as a decolourant gradually replaced that of antimony. Deliberate colouring could be achieved by the addition of different oxides; for example, copper oxide to create deep green glass or tin oxide to produce opaque white glass.

Coinage

The invention of coins as a medium of exchange probably derives directly from the use of ingots of electrum or silver bearing the stamp of the maker to guarantee the metal's quality. Earlier, ox-hide-shaped copper ingots found in Asia Minor and in Minoan Crete (c 1200 BC) may have been used as a kind of money. Earlier still, before metals came into general use, animal hides, or the cattle and sheep themselves may have been used for exchange: witness the Latin word for money, *pecunia,* which is derived from the word for cattle or sheep, *pecus.* In the period just before coinage was introduced, small iron rods or 'spits' were commonly used as money in Greece. In fact, these spits or *oboloi,* and a *dragma* of them (a handful), gave their names to the two most common denominations of Greek coins, the obol and the drachma.

The ancient writers tell us that the first coins were struck by Midas, King of Phrygia (c 738-696 BC). There is certainly a connection between this and the famous legend of Midas' "golden touch". Two kings of Lydia, Gyges (c 685-657 BC) and Croesus (c 560-546 BC), were both famous for their gold coins. The new art then spread westward from Asia Minor to Greece; archaeologists now are inclined to date the earliest Greek coins that have been discovered—those minted on the island of Aegina—to the end of the seventh century BC. Sometime during the sixth century BC, Corinth and Athens began to strike their own coins. The traditional date for the first true coins struck by the Romans is 289 BC.

Greek and Roman coins were universally made by a process of stamping or 'striking' as it is called. In this procedure, a small, pre-shaped pellet of metal is placed between two blocks of metal called 'dies'. Then, by means of sharp hammer blows, this pellet, or 'flan', takes on the impression in relief of the designs or letters that have been cut into the dies. The manufacture of the dies requires a technique of metal-working known as 'die-cutting', which was an extension of the art of gem and seal engraving, and was accomplished using a variety of small gravers, cutting wheels, and punches. This background of gem and seal engraving techniques at least partially accounts for the extraordinary beauty and fineness of detail of many of the high-relief designs that were a distinctive feature of the finest Greek and Roman coins.

Most of the flans in the Graeco-Roman world were prepared by casting in multiple clay moulds and sometimes the mould 'flash' is still visible at the edges of the coins. The lower, or anvil-die was made by engraving the coin device either directly into the anvil itself, or into a small block which was then set into the anvil. The flan was then hammered into the anvil-die by using a short bar, or punch-die, as it is called, and in the earliest coins this punch-die was not engraved with a design. This resulted in a coin with the design in relief on the anvil-die side (the obverse) and the incuse impression of the punch-die on the other (the reverse). Since, in this method of striking, the flan tended to spread out under the blows of the punch-die, Greek coins are often of irregular shape, and sometimes split at the edges. Both anvil- and punch-dies were commonly made of hardened bronze until about 400 BC; afterwards some were made of steel, since the harder metal was better for striking coins made of copper alloys.

As mentioned previously, the earliest coins had only the incuse, usually square, punch-die marks on the reverse, but in the middle of the sixth century BC, designs were beginning to be engraved on the reverse as well as the obverse. Perhaps the most famous example of an early reverse design is Athena's owl and olive branch on the tetradrachms of Athens, a type-design that remained unchanged throughout the city-state's history.

The basic process of striking coins described above was used throughout Graeco-Roman times, with few modifications. In Roman imperial times, the punch-die was frequently made in the form of a short, barrel-shaped bar, which was then set into an iron case. This had the advantage of better taking the force of the hammer blows, and in addition was probably made in such a way as to ensure that the obverse and reverse designs were in constant relation to each other. Although some ancient coins were cast in clay moulds rather than struck, they are relatively rare, and in most cases of cast coins one must suspect forgery.

A final word may be said on the materials of Greek and Roman coins. The earliest coins were made of a naturally occurring alloy of gold and silver which the Greeks called 'white gold' or electrum. They seem not to have known that this was an alloy, but accepted it as a distinct metal and had no regard for its proportionate content of gold and silver, which varied considerably. Its use in the Greek peninsula was largely superseded by silver in the sixth century BC, but Cyzicus and Lampsacus were producing important electrum *staters* in the fifth century. Since there was a plentiful supply of silver in and around the Greek peninsula, it quickly became the standard metal for coinage in that area. The Athenians were particularly fortunate in their discovery in the fifth century BC of rich silver ore deposits at Laurium in Attica. Gold as a material for coins did not become common until the fourth century BC but was used with some frequency thereafter. Both the gold and the silver used by the Greeks and Romans for striking coins was very pure; for example, the golden *aurei* of the Roman Emperor Augustus were .998 fine, and the tetradrachms of Athens in the fifth century BC were usually at least .983 fine.

The only other coin metals of importance in antiquity were bronze (a variety of tin-copper alloys) and brass (zinc-copper alloys). Bronze as a coin metal made its appearance in peninsular Greece quite late—about 400 BC in Athens—probably because the demand for coins of smaller denominations caused the silver coins to become too small for convenient handling. Rome, however, coined bronze from the beginning, basing its coinage on a bronze standard. The use of silver largely replaced bronze in the first century BC, but bronze coinage was revived and, together with brass, became important again under the Empire.

Plates

24

31

34

38

45

46

47

51

52

61

62

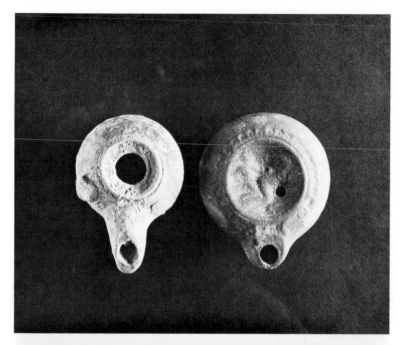

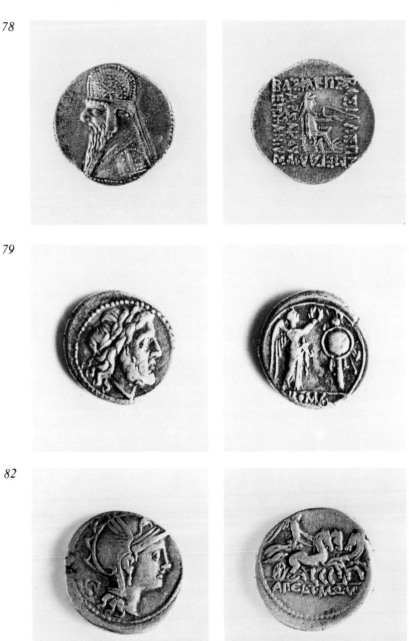

78

79

82

83

84

85

86

87

88

89

91

93

10,-/ 578/ 3850

8 N   nttc

This descriptive catalogue tells the story behind the Near Eastern and Classical exhibits on display in the Department of Classics at the University of Alberta.

The book describes the historical and archaeological background of the exhibits found at Tell-al-Ubaid, Iraq and highlights the skills aquired by this preliterate community which flourished during the fourth millennium BC. Similarly, artifacts discovered at Tell-en-Nasbeh, an Iron Age settlement six miles north of Jerusalem, are described and placed in their historical and archaeological context.

Short histories of Greek pottery, Roman glass, and lamps and coins of the ancient world are given and the technical processes used by the ancients are described.

Maps, drawings, and over 30 photographs help emphasize the fascination of everyday articles like a saucer lamp or a baby's feeding bottle used by peoples of civilizations that vanished thousands of years ago.